YOUR KNOWLEDGE HAS VALUE

- We will publish your bachelor's and master's thesis, essays and papers

- Your own eBook and book - sold worldwide in all relevant shops

- Earn money with each sale

Upload your text at www.GRIN.com
and publish for free

Bibliographic information published by the German National Library:

The German National Library lists this publication in the National Bibliography; detailed bibliographic data are available on the Internet at http://dnb.dnb.de .

This book is copyright material and must not be copied, reproduced, transferred, distributed, leased, licensed or publicly performed or used in any way except as specifically permitted in writing by the publishers, as allowed under the terms and conditions under which it was purchased or as strictly permitted by applicable copyright law. Any unauthorized distribution or use of this text may be a direct infringement of the author s and publisher s rights and those responsible may be liable in law accordingly.

Imprint:

Copyright © 2017 GRIN Verlag, Open Publishing GmbH
Print and binding: Books on Demand GmbH, Norderstedt Germany
ISBN: 9783668462861

This book at GRIN:

http://www.grin.com/en/e-book/359244/untouchable-god-as-the-indication-of-conventional-progressive-solutions

Rakibul Islam

Untouchable God as the indication of conventional progressive solutions

GRIN Publishing

GRIN - Your knowledge has value

Since its foundation in 1998, GRIN has specialized in publishing academic texts by students, college teachers and other academics as e-book and printed book. The website www.grin.com is an ideal platform for presenting term papers, final papers, scientific essays, dissertations and specialist books.

Visit us on the internet:

http://www.grin.com/

http://www.facebook.com/grincom

http://www.twitter.com/grin_com

Rakibul Islam

Research Scholar

Deptt. of English & Foreign Languages, CUH

Untouchable God as the indication of conventional progressive solutions

Abstract

"Progressivism" is an ideological, pragmatic system of thought grounded in solving problems and maintaining strong values within society. Progressive writers want to take some change in society or they want to provide some solution for the existing problems. When it comes to the case of caste system (untouchability), there are some conventional solutions given to eradicate caste and untouchability. These are intercaste marriage, providing education, upliftment of women, freedom of thought and expression, equal treatment, unequal opportunity etc. To a certain extent these solutions are effective in the society.

"Untouchable God: A Novel on Caste and Race" by Kancha Ilaiah (an Indian academician, writer, social, activist for dalit rights) is a portrayal of these ideas through the description of the life of Pariah and Saraswati. He also points out that the condition of upper caste women and makes a remark that their condition is also not different. This paper is an attempt to find the portrayal of these conventional progressive solutions prescribed for the upliftment of women and lower class.

Content

Abstract 1
Full Paper 2
Conclude 6
References 7

Full Paper

"Progressivism" is an ideological, pragmatic system of thought grounded in solving problems and maintaining strong values within society. Progressive writers want to bring some change in society or they want to provide some solution for the existing problems. The Indian Progressive Writers' Movement and Association first began after the publication of Angare (Burning Coals), a collection of short stories by Ahmed Ali, Sajjad Zaheer, Rashid Jehan and Mahmuduz Zafar in 1932 and its proscription by the British U. P. Government in 1933. A League of Progressive Authors was first announced by Ahmed Ali and Mamuduz Zafar in the leader of Allahabad dated April 5, 1933, which later expanded and became Indian Progressive Writers' Association.The progressive writer's association was established in London in 1935 by some Indian writers, intellectual with the encouragements and help of some British writers . The progressive writers of India established "The Progressive writers association" keeping in mind that radical change are taking place in Indian society so the new literature of India must deal with the basic problems of our existence to-day – the problems of hunger and poverty, social backwardness, and political subjection . It was in the Nanking Restaurant in central London that a group of writers, including Mulk Raj Anand, Sajjad Zaheer and Jyotirmaya Ghosh drafted a manifesto which stated their aims and objectives.

The untouchabity feature in the caste system is one of the cruelest features of the caste system. It is seen by many as one of the strongest racist phenomena in the world. In the Indian society people who worked in ignominious, polluting and unclean occupations were seen as polluting people and were therefore considered as Untouchables. The untouchable had almost no rights in the society. In deferent parts of India they were treated in different ways. In some regions the attitude towards the Untouchables was harsh and strict. The untouchable were seen as polluting people and their dwellings were at distance from the settlements of the four Varna communities. The untouchable were not allowed to touch people from the four varnas. They were not allowed to enter houses of the higher varnas. They were not allowed to enter the Temples. They were not allowed to use the same wells used by the Varnas. In public occasions they were compelled to sit at a distance from the four varnas. In regions where the attitude toward the untouchables were more severe, not only touching them was seen polluting, but also even a contact with their shadow was seen as polluting.

Kancha Ilaiah is an Indian academician, writer, social, activist for Dalit rights, born 5 October 1952 in Andhra Pradesh. He is not easy scholar to digest, with his brutal polemic against the Brahminical dominance of the Indian caste order. His latest assault, appropriately titled "Untouchable God: A Novel on Caste and Race", is a progression of the unique line of argument he has forwarded since he burst onto the Indian sociological scene with his seminal work "Why I am Not a Hindu: A Sudra Critique of Hindutva Philosophy, Culture and political Economy".

"Untouchable God", this witty-in-cheek novel that laughs at the foibles and hypocrisies of Brahmins and upper castes across India begins with a crime. Pariah , a dalit, is apparently beaten to death while walking about his village in the evening, allegedly for the crime of thinking about God, which might well lead to thoughts of equality……… six important men celebrate his death, which they had 'arranged'. They represent the remarkable Brahmins of India. Veda Shastry of Tamil Nadu (where the purest examples of exalted brahminhood are to be found) is the rightful leader. Namboodri of Kerala is from a caste that created the most perfect system of discrimination that the world has seen ; Ksihnamurthy of Karnataka and Appa Rao of Andhra Pradesh are slightly are moderate; Tilak of Maharashtra dreams of increasing discrimination while Banerjee of bangal believes he is above caste.

We can see in the novel, Untouchable God, how the upper caste Brahmins treats the Untouchables. At the same time Kancha Ilaiah point out some conventional progressive solutions. Pariah, an Untouchable man, a servant who started to thinking about his existence, role of God in creation but being a Untouchable, they are not allowed to think about God and he is killed by upper caste people.

'You bastard, how dare you think about soul, God and caste?' shouted an unknown voice. 'That means…Equality? You son of bitch, you too have begun to think! You too!' 'You bastards, stop thinking about God, you think about God. The moment thinks about God, you think about soul. Then you think about equality. All that nonsense'. (Ilaiah, page no 8 to 9).

Progressive is in the sense that Pariah started to think about God. Being the creation of same God why they are not allowed to touch God even they clean temples, clean the shits of the priests? He challenges the set tradition of Brahmins and started to think something new. On the other hand, Brahmins or the upper class people take it as a challenge to their identity. They know that if this lower caste people gets equal rights it will be very for them to survive in order to survive and live their live freely, they need power. Power is a concept which attracts everyone and everyone knows that power cannot be shared because it will reduce their importance in the society.

Education is medium which can help a person in getting his situation improved. Education of primary or higher level plays a vital role in setting a comfortable zone for any person. But for a country like India, which is divided into several castes and classes, it becomes very difficult to survive and getting education and in such situation when a particular group of society is abandoned from education. This situation is related to both sexes of Dalit class. In this story, Saraswati, who is a daughter of a Dalit, is not able to take education from priest. When her father asked the priest,

> "Punditji I have a daughter and I want to put her in the school. Will you please teach her? Whatever you charge I will pay'. Punditji replied 'What caste are you? Do you think we teach Shudra, Chandals, dogs and donkey? Who let you march into temple like this and ask me whether I would teach your low-born daughter-a girl, a damned bitch puppy! Get out! Out of this temple! take your defiling feet off my floor!"

This dialogue portrays the pathetic condition of the Dalit class which is not allowed to have education. In this dialogue, a Dalit father requests a priest to teach his daughter. He is also ready to pay full amount of fee to the priest. He wants to teach his daughter but the priest denies to teach his daughter. Pundit initially asks about his caste and then makes his mind whether to teach his daughter or not. He finds it against his will to teach a Dalit. He is scolds him and uses derogatory terms for him. He compares dalits with dogs and donkeys which shows his mentality about dalits. He rebukes him and orders him to leave his home. He takes him as an untouchable which can make him unholy. He also calls his daughter a bitch. He does not teach his daughter because she belongs to a dalit caste. He does not even think about her ability. Saraswati turns out to be a very intelligent girl. She further becomes very depressed by the orthodox beliefs of Hinduism and changes her religion. She adopts Mumtaj as her name. She learns Urdu in a Madrasa. But the poison of casteism does not leave her there; she is disturbed in life again and again. She marries to a Muslim boy named Hussain. He is brutally murdered because he had married a Hindu girl who had changed religion from Hinduism to Islam. It shows the rigidness of the Hindu religion. On one side, they were not ready to accept dalits and when these dalits were changing their religion, due to this rigidness, they were becoming the target of their hate. It shows the paradoxical nature of Hinduism, which is put forth by Kancha Ilaiah.

Kancha Ilaiah comes up with some solutions in his work. He talks about education for dalit as well as women. He also talks about the upliftment of women. He delivers the ideas of equal treatment of women in the society. He portrays the character of Saraswati who later on changes to Mumtaj is a well educated girl. She gets humiliated initially by the upper caste/class men of the society and she changes her religion. If she would have got equal opportunity and behavior she would have been flourished more than what she was. This society should be flexible where everyone can get equal chance to prove his/her talent.

Feelings are the mirror of one's character. If one has good feelings, he moves towards good or right way. On the other hand, bad feelings take a man toward wrong side of the society. Feelings are very important in one's life whether they are good or bad. But when these feelings are curtailed, their life becomes helpless. Basu is a character which wants to develop himself but his father becomes a hurdle in his development. He wants good relationships with dalit people of the society but his father takes it as an attack to their identity. He marries him against his will and tries to make him engaged in day to day life.

In this book, Kancha Ilaiah also depicts a character which does not accept the social norms. She rejects the idea of Sati Pratha and wants to live her life completely. This point somewhere put forth the idea of progressivism. We find this character as a changing aspect of the novel. She puts forth the idea of liberty, life and progressivism.

Conclude

Kancha Ilaiah is a progressive writer who puts forth new ideas of which forces the readers to change their thinking about dalits and subjugated people of the society. In this book, he comes up with changing ideas. He challenges the social norms and tries to break them. He shows the new dimensions which leads human welfare.

References: Ilaiah, Kancha. "Untouchable God: A Novel on Caste and Race". Kolkata: SAMYA,2013. Print.

YOUR KNOWLEDGE HAS VALUE

- We will publish your bachelor's and master's thesis, essays and papers

- Your own eBook and book - sold worldwide in all relevant shops

- Earn money with each sale

Upload your text at www.GRIN.com and publish for free